799
notrade

NATURE'S SECRETS

MARI FRIEND

BROCKHAMPTON PRESS

First published by Brockhampton Press Ltd
20 Bloomsbury Street
London WC1B 3QA

© Brockhampton Press Ltd, 1998
© Mari Friend (text and illustrations), 1998

ISBN 1 86019 412 5

Designed and conceived by Savitri Books Ltd

INTRODUCTION

It is fascinating to watch small animals living their varied life cycles. Their secret world of courtship, mating, reproduction, growth, hunting and defence is being enacted all the time, almost under our noses. There is no need to go to far-flung places to observe the minor miracles performed by mother nature: they are there for all to see, if only we take the time and trouble to pause and watch. Over thousand of years plants and animals have evolved a myriad of ways in which to survive extremes of climate, to foil predators and ensure the survival of their species. Sometimes these patterns of behaviour are difficult to interpret and need some words of explanation from someone who has watched the whole procedure and who has begun to understand its complexity.

Mari Friend is just one of these privileged people. Despite her father's early prounouncement that 'only vicars' daughters become naturalists', she went on to study biology and horticulture. In 1980, she returned to live in her native Yorkshire where, with the help of Countryside Commission grants, she and her husband started the Bracken Hall Countryside Centre – one of the chief attractions being a wildlife room in which adults and children could follow the fascinating or strange life cycles of water creatures in tanks, and of bees in an observation hive.

She is the author of *Small Wonder – A new Approach to Understanding Nature*, a book which won the Sir Peter Kent Conservation Book Prize for 1991 and went into several foreign editions. She also wrote *Winter Survival – Nature's Ways of Coping with the Cold*, *A Countryside Daybook* and a children's book: *Discovering Nature's Secrets*. This latest book presents fascinating extracts from her writing, which are, as her previous works, enhanced by her magical illustrations.

The Passion Flower & the Hummingbird – the Perfect Partnership

In order to produce fruits, many plants depend on birds for cross-pollination and the flowers must advertise their attractions if they are to encourage animals to visit them. The hummingbird who feeds on nectar performs this function for a variety of flowers. A typical hummingbird flower is one that opens by day, with the petals arranged in an open rosette or an overhanging hood; it must produce copious amounts of nectar but have no scent. The hummingbird is a tiny creature with a long, slender and pointed beak or bill that enables him to probe various nectar sources; whether it be the long nectar tubes of passion flowers or the short tubes of daisy-like flowers.

The Andean sword-billed hummingbird is a small bird with a bill measuring 83mm (3.25 inches) in length. This unwieldy appendage is used with great skill to probe the deep nectar tubes of *Passiflora mixta*, which are 114mm (4.25 inches) long – too long for the beak alone to be effective, but the bird uses its tongue to reach the base of the nectaries. This same long bill is dexterously put to work in building a nest and for delicately feeding the hummingbird's young.

When it wants to feed from the passion flower, the hummingbird pushes its head close to the flower in order to reach the nectaries at the base of the petals. After feeding in this way, it leaves the flower, carrying away a dusting of pollen grains on its head; the next flower it visits may trap these pollen grains on a sticky receptive stigma – and so cross-pollination will have been carried out and the hummingbird will have earned its nectar. The passion flower illustrated opposite is *Passiflora caerulea*, a native of Brazil. It is a climbing plant with fascinating flowers. The spectacular blooms measure 7.5cm (3 inches) across and have five sepals

and five petals. All ten structures are greeny-white in colour; each sepal carries a little spur at the tip, while the petals are simply rounded. Around the centre of the flower there is a fringe of radiating filaments called the corona; this is banded in blue, white and dark

When South America was newly colonized by Spain, the Catholic missionaries saw features in the plant which they interpreted as symbols of Christ's crucifixion, so they used it when teaching the native people the gospel. The ten tepals – sepals and petals – represented ten of the Apostles; Judas was discounted because he betrayed Christ and Peter was left out because he denied knowing Him. The corona was thought to be like the Crown of Thorns; the five anthers represented the five wounds made in Christ's body, while the three stigmas were like the nails that were driven into His body to nail Him to the Cross. The ovary, which is at the base of the rising central stalk, was said to be the shape of the jar of vinegar offered to Jesus by a Roman soldier. The five-lobed leaves and the whip-like tendrils represented the hands and scourges of His persecutors.

Seeing Red

I have been interested in the colour red for a long time, because of its power to attract and repel, to be dangerous – as in red for danger – yet, according to folklore and among some animals, to have protective properties.

The hard red forewings of some ladybirds warn would-be predators that the ladybird tastes nasty; young, inexperienced predators often try to eat these attractively coloured insects, but find them so bitter that they spit them out and avoid them in future. So the ladybird's red colouring warns the predator of danger and protects the useful insect.

The robin's red breast is used to good effect when another robin enters his territory; the defending robin pushes out his breast to make it conspicuous and fluffs out all his other feathers too so that he looks as big as possible. When an unattached female robin comes along in spring, the male, who has defended his territory against all comers throughout the winter, behaves in exactly the same way to the female as he did to any other intruder; but the female is attracted by the expanse of red breast and stands her ground, singing back to her intended mate. After a day or two of sparring, she is accepted.

Some of the red fruits we see in the hedgerow are poisonous and we do well to be cautious about eating some of them. White bryony and black bryony – *Bryonia dioica* and *Tamus communis* – have red globular fruits which, if eaten in quantity, make a person very ill. The red pendulous fruits of the woody nightshade, *Solanum dulcamara*, slow down the heart rate and lower both blood pressure and body temperature. Lords and ladies and cuckoo pint, *Arum italicum* and *Arum maculatum*, have orange-scarlet berries which can make one feel quite unwell; while the orange-red seeds of stinking iris, *Iris foetidissima*, contain a poison which is a severe irritant on the alimentary tract. But the red fruits of holly, rowan, cherry, tomato, apple and raspberry are perfectly edible and the red colour seems to be a signal to the birds to come and eat.

Under the birch tree, among the fallen leaves, fly agaric fungi, *Amanita muscaria*, (see opposite), spread their red caps flecked with white. This fungus is so called because it contains toxins which can stun and kill flies. It is just one of a number of fungi which induce hallucinations when eaten; it is not advisable to try them, as serious physical damage may result. But fly agaric was probably used in the ceremonials of ancient religions to induce ritual hallucinations.

Honeysuckle

Honeysuckle flowers open in early summer and their heady scent makes walking along the hedgerows a wonderful experience. They are often seen next to the white, trumpet-like flowers of the hedge bindweed, as illustrated opposite. Strips of honeysuckle are often used by the dormouse to weave her oval nest, although grass may also be employed. Honeysuckle is a plant of mixed deciduous woodland and hedgerows, where it twines its clockwise way so tightly that it can make barley sugar twists of the stems of young trees. You may have seen walking sticks made from stems that have been twisted in this way. Honeysuckle produces a profusion of flowers, and their main pollinators are hawkmoths and bumble bees. Early grey moths and gold spangle moths put their eggs on honeysuckle leaves, as do the clearwing and the broad-bordered bee hawkmoths and white admiral butterflies.

Butterfly and moths

There is no distinct division between butterflies and moths, except that butterflies fly by day. They are some of the most colourful and fascinating visitors to any garden. They all have clubbed antennae and most have bright wings. Butterflies usually fold their wings together when at rest, while moths tend to flatten theirs. Many moths are dull in colour and nocturnal in habit, but there are also those which are bright in colour and which fly by day – burnet moths, for example.

Butterflies and moths undergo four stages of development:

egg — larva — pupa — imago (adult)

When a larva or caterpillar hatches, its first food is often its own egg shell, then it looks for plant food. Usually the eggs will have been laid on or near the specific food of the species. The caterpillar has powerful biting jaws with which it feeds voraciously. The body has three pairs of walking legs and no more than five pairs of clasping legs with hooks, which enable the caterpillar to cling. The segmented body may be covered with hairs; it may have spines, or it may be coloured to camouflage or 'warn' predators.

The caterpillar grows rapidly and as its outer skin does not stretch, this has to be shed; caterpillars usually have five or six instars (phases between each moult). When the caterpillar is fully grown, it chooses a suitable site for pupation; some, including many moth caterpillars burrow into the soil or spin a silken cocoon; many butterfly larvae suspend their pupa case from a pad of silk spun on a leaf or twig. The caterpillar sheds its final skin and enters the pupa stage.

The word 'pupa' comes from the Latin for doll or puppet and many moth pupae do indeed look like a doll wrapped in a shawl. 'Chrysalis' is from a Greek word meaning gold and refers to the metallic spots which can be seen on the cases of many pupating butterflies.

The length of the period of pupation varies according to the species and the time of year. One day when the weather is fine and the temperature is right, the adult insect inflates and bursts the pupa case. It climbs out slowly and laboriously; its wings are crumpled and flattened and need to be expanded. This is a highly vulnerable time for the insect.

Butterflies and moths have to warm up their flight muscles before take-off. Butterflies' wings act as solar panels, which is why few butterflies are seen flying in dull weather. Moths usually warm up by beating their wings rapidly. Both butterflies and moths couple up their wings on either side of

the body so that they beat as one, giving greater strength and lifting power.

For adult butterflies and moths, the main objective in life is reproduction. So males and females of the same species must find each other in order to mate and effect fertilization.

Unfertilized females secrete a characteristic odour from their abdominal glands; the substance of this odour is a pheromone, an external chemical message carried on the air. Any males in the area will be led by this scent and locate the virgin female; males emit sexual odours too, but these are released to induce the female to copulate.

During the summer months, specialized sexual display flights often take place, with the male fluttering round the female in a complicated dance. In late summer or early spring there is more urgency to the proceedings and the courtship ritual is abandoned.

The external male reproductive organs are rather like tweezers which grasp the tip of the female's abdomen; pairing takes place in a back-to-back position. During copulation, spermatophores – sacks of sperm – are deposited within a membraneous receptacle inside the female; these provide a sperm bank upon which the female draws to fertilize the eggs as they mature inside her ovaries.

When mating has taken place, the female has to find the caterpillar's food plant; the eggs inside her make her heavy as she flies low over the vegetation. There are tiny sense organs at the tips of her feet which respond only to certain chemicals and confirm that she has chosen the correct plant species on which to lay her eggs.

A Predator and its Prey – Ladybirds & Aphids

Ladybirds are beetles, and most of the 45 species found in Britain and northern Europe are predators who feed on aphids, scale insects and other sedentary, thin-skinned invertebrates. Among these the ladybird adults and larvae wander at will, feeding on the creatures that damage plants.

After mating, the female ladybird lays her eggs on a leaf in the vicinity of a colony of aphids, so the young find food as soon as they hatch. Ladybird eggs look very much like the eggs of cabbage white butterflies at first glance; but look at them through a magnifying glass and you will see that ladybird eggs are yellow and shiny, while cabbage white eggs are yellow and sculptured. Most ladybird larvae are curious blue-black creatures with yellow spots. They consume hundreds of aphids during their three weeks as larvae, then they pupate in a sheltered place on the plant. About six days later the adult ladybird emerges, very pale and soft, before the front wings harden and darken into bright colours.

Not all ladybirds are red with black spots. Some are black with red spots, some yellow or orange with dark spots or splodges. Ladybirds are the gardener's friend as they eat so many plants pests. They, on the other hand, enjoy a natural protection: a reflex bleeding mechanism to alarm and warn predators. This mechanism also operates if they are roughly handled; the 'bleeding' takes the form of an unpleasant-smelling, orange-coloured substance which oozes from their joints. Birds do not seem to like the taste of ladybirds, and if a bird eats one, by chance or experiment, it rarely repeats the performance.

Ladybirds' favourite prey – the aphid – is a plant bug. There are many species of aphids, the most common being the blackfly and the greenfly. Aphids feed by piercing the tissues

of a plant with a needle-like mouth part called a proboscis; sap is extracted from the plant by suction.

Examine an aphid under a magnifying glass and you will find a pair of tubes, like car exhausts, projecting from a spot near the end of its abdomen. These tubes exude a waxy substance which covers the aphid's body and probably prevents dehydration.

In late autumn, male and female aphids mate. Eggs are laid on to the twigs of trees or shrubs, where they overwinter before hatching into wingless females in the spring. These females in turn give birth to live daughters by a process called parthenogenesis, which means virgin birth – the eggs are not fertilized by a male. Some of the young have wings and are able to fly to other plants, so spreading the population around – a familiar and dreaded sight to a gardener. Each female gives birth to about fifty daughters during her short life, but during October some males are born. Mating then takes place and overwintering eggs are laid. A mild winter ensures a larger population of aphids, as well as of their predators.

What is a Hedgerow?

A hedgerow is a long corridor along which many animals and plants spread themselves out across the countryside, linking one fragment of woodland with another. In this way, the plants and animals of the ancient woodlands have not been entirely lost. Over the centuries, many plants and animals have gradually adapted to man-made countryside; it is possible that in the new pattern of copses, fields, hedgerows, gardens and houses some wildlife may have become even more successful. For example, birds such as the robin, blackbird and thrush could be more common now than when they lived in a purely woodland habitat; while the seed-eating chaffinch, yellowhammer and greenfinch must find more food in a field of corn or stubble than they ever did in the ancient woodlands.

Hedgerows offer a particularly rich habitats for wildlife because they combine the features of a woodland with those of open fields; while a hedge with a ditch and bank is often home to plants and animals once more usually found in habitats which are rapidly disappearing, such as marshland and old pasture.

The constant growth and annual cutting of a hedge means that the habitat continually changes, encouraging a great diversity of species. A lot depends on when the hedge is cut, as a matter of a few weeks can greatly influence the floral composition and the insects who depend on the hedgerow. A look at the sections of a hedgerow will give some idea of the diversity of life to be found there.

Hawthorn, or quickthorn, *Crataegus monogyna*, is a tree of glades and woodland edges, where it grows to about 12 metres (40 ft) in height. It is probably the most common hedgerow plant; the word for hedge is based on the Saxon name for the fruit of the hawthorn – hag or haw.

About 150 insects are associated with the hawthorn; these insects also visit other members of the family Rosaceae which grow along the hedgerow. Hawthorn flowers produce nectar and attract flies, beetles and various bees in late spring. Of the many insects found in association with hawthorn, 80 or more are moth larvae; it is fortunate that they are able to eat other plants, too, or the hawthorn would be defoliated regularly!

Hawthorn berries are eaten by birds and by small mammals who live in the hedge bottom. Birds nest in the hawthorn, use it as a roost and hunt among the spiky branches. These birds and small mammals are hunted by birds of prey, foxes, stoats and weasels. Shrews hunt for invertebrates on the hedge bank. Most predators leave shrews alone, not liking the smell extruded from their stink glands; but owls take them, so they must not mind the smell.

Bluebells on a hedge bank indicate that this was a piece of old woodland. The flowers are pollinated by bees and bee flies; bee flies are true flies that look like fat bees. Stitchwort and red campion are other woodland plants which are often found along a hedgerow; foxgloves are plants of woodland edges and glades which are pollinated by bumble bees.

Goldfinches

On my walks I often see goldfinches exploring the dead heads, searching for any seeds that may still be found on them. Through the autumn, family groups of these colourful birds hang on to thistle heads, burdocks and hardheads (see page 27), swinging to and fro as they probe for seeds with their substantial but finely pointed bills. Goldfinches frequent gardens, allotments, wasteland, farmland, scrubland, sand dunes, salt marshes and roadside verges; when they are disturbed they rise, twittering, the liquid notes of their calls sounding like a chime of tiny bells – no wonder the collective noun for goldfinches is 'charm'. A goldfinch's bill enables it to extract seeds from deep inside the heads of teasel; if you examine a teasel head you will see that this operation needs an expert technician to carry it out. Watch carefully and you will see how a goldfinch pulls the seed head forward and clamps the stem down firmly under its feet, in order to extract seeds from the head. Thistles are the favourite food of goldfinches; they eat the seeds from these and other plants through until late autumn. Then they begin to concentrate on fallen seeds on the ground and the seeds of

low-growing plants, leaving the seed heads on taller stems for later in the winter, when snow might cover the ground and the shorter-stemmed plants.

Badgers, foxes and squirrels

Badgers are found in many countries, the animal known as the European badger having a range extending from the British Isles throughout Europe – apart from the far north – into Japan and southern China. The American badger is found from south-western Canada to central Mexico. The two species have a similar life-cycle.

Badgers give birth to their young following a period of prolonged inactivity in winter. In Britain, this usually occurs during January or February: it may be a little earlier in the south, while in the north and east it may be a little later. Up to five youngsters are born; they are blind and helpless and they snuggle together in the deep bed of straw, hay, bracken and dead leaves which makes up their cosy nest. It is important that the nursery chamber in the badgers' sett is well furnished with large quantities of insulating material, as this helps the cubs to retain their body heat, particularly when their mother has left them alone to forage for food to maintain her own strength and keep up her milk supply.

A few weeks after the cubs are born, the badger sow mates again. She may do so several times throughout the following summer, but February seems to be the peak time for sexual excitement. But instead of the blastocysts – developing eggs – being promptly implanted in the wall of the uterus, they remain free in the womb until the following November or December, when the womb lining becomes receptive. When the eggs do become embedded, they begin to grow rapidly, a placenta is formed and the foetuses are linked to the

Colourful goldfinches feeding on thistle heads and grass seeds.

mother's blood supply, which carries food and oxygen to the developing cubs.

Badgers eat a great deal of food in autumn, then they sleep for long periods, remaining in a state of semi-dormancy for several weeks. It is thought that during this time hormones are released which trigger the lining of the womb into becoming receptive.

Red foxes are solitary animals for much of the year, but when they carry out their courtship during January and February, the high-pitched calls and screams of their love songs echo unforgettably through the frosty air.

During the mating season, a dog fox may hunt with the vixen of his choice, searching for voles, mice, rats, rabbits, hares and birds. The red fox, like the badger, eats large quantities of insects and earthworms; opportunist feeders of this sort prey on anything they can catch and this flexible diet allows foxes to thrive in unlikely environments. They are often seen in suburbs, and increasingly in city centres, where they raid dustbins and consume anything remotely edible. Walking with a light, almost soundless tread, the fox travels long distances, usually by night, hunting for food; in winter snowy tracks often reveal just how far it has travelled.

Popular tradition portrays the fox as a ruthless hunter, capable of killing far more animals than it can eat. There is some truth in this belief: when a fox gets into a situation where there is a lot of prey that cannot escape – such as a hen house – it will often kill every bird. The reason for this is that the fox's killing instincts are triggered by movement. In the wild, if a group of animals is attacked, many will scatter and most will escape; then, when the victim lies dead and still, the fox is satisfied. But in the confines of a hen house the birds cannot escape and their terrified fluttering stimulates the fox into killing again and again; not for sport, but as a

response to the instinct to kill prey whenever the opportunity arises. If a fox did not do this in the wild, it would soon starve.

It was once thought that red and grey squirrels hibernated through the winter, but this is not so, both species being active during many of the short winter days. Squirrels stay curled up in their warm nests, known as dreys, when the weather is very cold, wet or windy, and when there is deep snow or icy conditions; however, they are able to go without food for only two or three days, after which time they leave the drey to forage even in severe weather. This is where their secret hoards come in useful – if the squirrels can remember the hiding-places they chose in the autumn!

Grey squirrels live mainly in broad-leaved woodlands and it is easy to spot their dreys high in the trees; they are usually built away from the trunk, balanced in a fork or between thick branches. The dreys of both grey and red squirrels are rounded, about the size of a football, with a side entrance; they are made of close-knit twigs and the pliant stems of ivy and honeysuckle, and lined with leaves and moss. In winter the grey squirrel's coat is thick; it is yellow-brown on the head and flanks and silver-grey elsewhere, while the conspicuous bushy tail is dark grey with a white fringe.

The grey squirrel was introduced to Britain and Ireland in the nineteenth century from North America, where it is found in the hardwood forests of eastern Canada and the United States. from Ontario and New Brunswick down to Florida. Black squirrels, a dark-coloured or melanistic form rather than a different species, are commonly found in some parts of this range. Black squirrels are occasionally seen in the British Isles, but the dark colour doesn't seem to worry either animal, as grey and black interbreed successfully.

Red squirrels are smaller than their grey cousins; they are the only diurnal tree squirrel in continental Europe, living wherever there are coniferous forests and broad-leaved woodlands, particularly in beech woods. In most parts of Europe there are black forms of the red squirrel, just as there are melanistic grey squirrels. The two forms occur together in the same population and interbreed; the ratio of dark to red animals varies from place to place. In autumn, throughout most of its range,the red squirrel moults to a dull greyish-brown, it develops prominent ear tufts and the tail becomes bushier and darker; but in northern Scandinavia the entire winter coat may fade to almost pure silver-grey. The ears and tail of both squirrel species are very important balancing organs, besides being expressive signalling devices; for example, the ears are laid back as a sign of aggression and stick up as a sign of defence.

Red squirrels spend most of their time in the tree-tops, coming down to ground level only to search for windfall cones or fungi. Having found food, the squirrel seeks out a tree stump or rock on which to sit, so that it can maintain a look-out while eating.

Both red and grey squirrels have two breeding seasons: one in summer, June to August, the other in winter, December to March. The squirrels born early in the year have a greater chance of surviving their first full winter, as by the time the cold weather arrives they are bigger than the summer brood and better able to fend for themselves. Squirrel courtship rituals involve display and racing and chasing among the branches, along the ground and up the trees. The male that first catches the female mates with her, and the other males then leave her alone. The female repairs or enlarges a drey, or sometimes uses a hollow tree, for her nursery nest, lining it with soft, warm material such as grass, moss, shredded bark, and feathery seed heads and sheep's wool if these are available. There is a gestation period of five to six weeks before three to six young are born, blind, deaf and naked.

Female squirrels are good mothers and care for their babies for about sixteen weeks, by which time the young are completely independent.

Birds on the Bark

Woodpeckers, nuthatches and treecreepers, the birds which find their food on tree trunks, are highly adapted climbers. They cling vertically and use their tails as a prop; only birds which forage regularly on the tree trunks have stiffened tail feathers, sometimes with the tips of the two central veins missing to leave a spike, which acts as a grip on the bark.

Woodpeckers, in particular, rely on the two central tail feathers for support and delay shedding them whey they moult until the replacement feathers have grown. It is essential to have strong grip when chiselling into bark or poking into crevices to extricate some choice invertebrate, so the birds which are seen on tree bark have sharp, curved claws and powerful thigh muscles. Woodpeckers have two toes facing forward and two behind to give maximum grip; this arrangement is quite unusual in birds.

The 'tree-climbing' birds progress up and down trunks and along branches by pressing their tail down firmly and hopping. The usual pattern of the search for food is to hop up the trunk of one tree and then fly to the base of the next, but nuthatches are able to move upwards and horizontally; they are also so often seen coming down a tree head first that it was once commonly thought that they even roosted upside down!

Woodpeckers chisel into wood to search for insect larvae, woodlice and other invertebrates which hide behind loose bark or in the timber. A woodpecker's skull is especially

The bird on the left is a
a treecreeper, the one on the
right is a nuthatch.

thick-walled to absorb the impact of the striking hammer blows; and an amazingly long tongue probes the chiselled holes to reach the wood-boring grubs within.

The nuthatch wedges nuts into crevices in a tree, a post or a wall to hold them steady for hammering open; while the treecreeper's long, slender, finely pointed beak delicately picks tiny items of food from their hiding place in the fissures of bark.

The treecreeper is so well camouflaged that the first time I ever spotted one in its winter roost, it made me jump. It was in an oval cavity, about the size of a hen's egg, in a tree trunk. It had snuggled vertically into the hollow with its back to the world and all its feathers fluffed out for maximum warmth.

Short Day – Long Night

As temperatures fall, so do the leaves. For centuries, country people have watched the behaviour of trees in autumn closely and used it to predict the following winter's weather: 'October with green leaves means a severe winter' is one of many pieces of folk wisdom, most of which seem to spread gloom and despondency. I expect this is because few of us look forward to the short days, long nights and cold of the winter. But when the rich colours of summer begin to dissipate in autumn, there is a burst of splendour as green leaves change to gold, orange, russet or deep crimson. Some trees are more beautiful in autumn than at any other time of the year, their lofty crowns reminding us of the brilliant colour of captured sunsets or perhaps the flickering fires of frosty nights.

But why do so many trees change their leaf colour in autumn, and why do the leaves then fall? The answer lies with the invisible biological clock that all plants and animals

have. It measures the length of the day – or night. So, at the spring equinox, when day and night are the same length, plants and animals know that it is time to grow or breed, because a long cold period has just passed and the days are lengthening. At the autumn equinox, after a season of growth and fruitfulness, the days are shortening and it is time to prepare for winter. For many trees, as we shall see, this means losing their leaves. Throughout Britain, Europe and North America, all broad-leaves trees and a few coniferous ones such as larches and deciduous cypresses (*Taxodium* spp.) shed their leaves in autumn.

All land plants release water vapour into the air by a process called transpiration. This can take place from any exposed part of the plant, but the greatest water loss is through the pores in the leaves which are known as stomata. The rate of transpiration varies according to atmospheric conditions and the make-up of the plant.

The green colour we see in plants is caused by two closely related pigments, chlorophyll 'a' and chlorophyll 'b'. These pigments are able to form only in the presence of light, with a favourable temperature – not lower than 2°C (36°F) or higher than 40°C (104°F) – and with an adequate supply of water and minerals and carbohydrates manufactured by the plant.

Chlorophyll in living cells is necessary for the process called photosynthesis to take place. this is the method by which plants manufacture organic foods from simple inorganic compounds using light energy. The other essential factors for photosynthesis are sunlight, carbon dioxide and water. The process produces oxygen, carbohydrates and water vapour, all of which are essential for life on earth.

In autumn, when the days become shorter and temperatures fall, a layer of specialized cells begins to form at the base of each deciduous leaf. The cells behind this layer become corky and impervious to water. The normal transportation of materials in and out of the leaf is impeded, and this interferes with the formation of chlorophyll. Chlorophyll is constantly being used up, and when the supplies required for its renewal run out, the leaves lose their green colour. When the green pigment disappears, any other colouring that may be in the leaves can be seen. Yellow chemicals called flavenoids are always found in association with chlorophyll in leaves, protecting the chlorophyll from too much sunlight, so when the green colour is no longer produced, the yellow becomes visible. Trees such as sycamore, birch horse chestnut, black poplar and its hybrids have predominantly yellow leaves in autumn.

Some leaves contain anthocyanins, chemical compounds which give the colours red, blue and violet-purple. These colours are not usually present in the leaf during the summer, as flavenoids are, but form as the leaves begin to wilt. Often the leaves which develop the greatest intensity of red are rich in sugars. These show up particularly well on bright autumn days after a cold snap, as frost traps the sugars in the leaves. This explains why some trees which have red leaves in autumn are particularly spectacular in certain years; look out for Virginia creeper, red and silver maples, sumachs and some oaks, especially pin oak and scarlet oak. In New England, where early frosts followed by warm spells commonly occur and deciduous trees are abundant, the glorious reds of autumn are rightly famous. The forests of Canada are spectacular, too. I revelled in these one autumn , then returned home to Britain, where the golden leaves of the beeches and the yellow needles of the larches were just as lovely, if less flamboyant.

Let us return to the specialized cells which form at the base of each deciduous leaf, causing the colour to change.

The cells form a layer across the area where the leaf stalk joins the twig. This is called the abscission layer. The cells nearest the twig make a corky layer and those nearest the leaf stalk are thin and loosely packed. The valuable carbohydrates which have been manufactured in the leaf are in soluble form and are normally passed from the leaf into the plant through the vascular tissue. Waste substances pass from the plant into the leaf for excretion. Gradually the abscission layer thickens and blocks the vascular tissue, so that water and minerals are no longer able to enter the leaf from the plant. The leaf changes colour and begins to die.

The cells in the leaf stalk degenerate and the vascular strands, which once carried the plant's water supplies into the leaf and the carbohydrates out, finally break, so that the leaf falls. The corky layer of cells near the twig now protects the plant from water loss and prevents disease-producing organisms from entering..

The shape of the scar left by the fallen leaf is specific to a given species of plant. For example, the horse chestnut tree is so called because the scar left by a fallen leaf is horseshoe-shaped; the vein scars even leave marks that look like the nails of a shoe. You will find leaf scars on all twigs; those of horse chestnut, sweet chestnut, ash and sycamore are probably the easiest to examine.

Cuckoo pint

Arum maculatum, cuckoo pint (see opposite), is constructed to lure and trap small flies such as owl midges. Flowers adapted to pollination by flies usually smell unpleasantly of sweat, urine, excretion or bad meat and they are dull in colour. The true flowers of the cuckoo pint are hidden from view inside the greenish-yellow spathe, which is a modified leaf. Inside the spathe there is a purple or yellow club-like

structure called a spadix. Near the base of the spadix you will find a circle of downward-pointing hairs. Below these hairs, tiny male flowers encircle the spadix base; and below these the slightly larger female flowers cluster. The spadix releases a slight warmth as well as a smell of urine; these two factors attract the midges.

When an owl midge lands on the inner side of the spathe, or spadix, it is probably carrying pollen from another cuckoo pint flower. The spathe walls are slippery with oil droplets and the suckers on the midge's feet can't grip; so the insect falls down through the circle of hairs, past the male flowers, and lands on the female flowers. the midge wanders around the flowers, inadvertently rubbing pollen on to the sticky stigmatic surfaces, but unable to leave the chamber at the base of the spathe because the hairs prevent escape. When the female flowers are pollinated, they exude a drop of nectar which seems to make the midge happy.

During the course of the day, the pollinated stigmas wither; when this happens, the anthers open and shower the midge with pollen. When the pollen is shed, the hairs barring the way out wither and the spathe becomes wrinkled and easy to climb. The midge thankfully climbs towards light and freedom – probably to be lured into the next cuckoo pint plant along the hedgerow!

The warming of the spadix and the production of the scent are at their height during the first afternoon and evening that the spathes are open. The number of insects caught inside the chamber at this time can be surprisingly large.

A River Walk in Winter

Most birds are able to survive short periods of harsh weather by utilizing the fat deposits laid down under their skin in

autumn, but few can withstand severe winter conditions for long. Waterside birds probably suffer most when their food supplies are sealed below a layer of ice.

I count myself lucky when I see the resident kingfisher on my walks by the river. Kingfishers live along streams with high banks, canals, ponds, lakes and flooded gravel pits, wherever there is a good supply of sticklebacks and minnows. A kingfisher often sits motionless on a perch in a strategic position overlooking the water; or sometimes it may hover over a pool, watching for the movement of a small fish, a water beetle or an aquatic insect larva. Suddenly there is a flash of iridescent blue-green and the small rainbow-coloured bird drops into the water, reappearing in seconds with its prey in its beak. It beats sticklebacks against its perch until they are dead and the dorsal spines lie flat along the back. Fish are always eaten head first, as eating a fish tail first would force the gills and scales back and choke the kingfisher, so it juggles with its victims to ensure they go down the right way.

Male and female kingfishers occupy different territories out of the breeding season; the sexes look alike, but the male's bill is all black while the female has an orange-red lower mandible. During harsh winters many kingfishers die of cold and starvation; but a worse threat to this beautiful bird is from water pollution and the removal of river-bank trees, which afford perches, privacy and nesting possibilities among the root systems.

The dipper is a stocky, thrush-shaped bird of fast-flowing streams. All through the winter its clear voice can be heard, warbling a song of territorial possession. One of my favourite walks, at all times of the year, takes me along a river-bank where I can watch a dipper fishing. It stands on a boulder with water foaming all around, curtseying to the river before it plunges in, diving through the water using its short wings

as fins. It is wonderful to stand on a bridge and see this dark bird walking into the current under the river, wings angled, searching for the invertebrates adapted to life in fast-flowing water. Up bobs the dipper (see below), firmly gripping a stonefly nymph or a caddis larva, blinking the water from its eyes with a white membranous eyelid. Dippers and kingfishers both have soft, dense plumage for insulation; but when icicles hang from the bending trees and water plants are ringed with ice, how I shiver for these birds that have to dive into the cold winter waters in order to live!

Grey wagtails (opposite page) share the same stretch of water as the dipper; it is an area of boulders and deep pools just below a weir, where the river quietens and becomes more peaceful. Despite their sombre name, grey wagtails are bright birds in every way: they are nimble, with tails that twitch continually as they search for insects; they have elegant, streamlined bodies, grey-blue above and lemon yellow below. Males have a black throat-patch in the breeding season, but after the autumn moult the sexes look alike. In winter the birds become more

gregarious and groups roost together for warmth. Some grey wagtails leave their usual haunts in late autumn and may be seen around sewage farms and cress beds, where more insects are to be found, but they are seldom far from a tumbling stream or a weir.

Mallards inhabit all parts of the river. These ducks are found in ponds in parks in towns and villages, in gravel pits, reservoirs, lakes, estuaries and salt marshes. Just in case their numbers need swelling, immigrants arrive from western Europe to overwinter in Britain. In autumn the mallards begin to pair up. October is a good month to watch the displays, when the drakes, splendid in their breeding plumage, swim low in the water, flicking their heads, jabbing their bills into the water, splashing and showing off their black, curled tail feathers. When the ducks approach, the drakes often respond by rearing out of the water, stretching their necks and whistling. A duck will choose the drake which, in her eyes, is displaying most vigorously; she bobs her head to one side and swims close by him. The rejected males begin to squabble and lunge at each other with their bills; this often frightens the duck, which may fly off, followed by several amorous drakes. Mating takes place in November, and once the pair are bonded they stay close together within the group or flock.

I think herons must have endless patience. I pass one most days on my walk; it stands motionless, 'shoulders' hunched, bayonet-shaped bill pointing towards the shallow water, a solitary grey sentinel waiting for a fish, perhaps an eel, to swim by. Many herons die in severe winters, when ice prevents them from catching food, but many more die when their feeding ground becomes polluted by toxic chemicals, as when agricultural spray run-off seeps into the watery habitat. Sometimes I startle the heron; then it slowly and majestically takes to its broad, rounded wings, flapping away to soar and glide and come to rest further up the river.

Wading Birds

Estuaries all over Europe give vital refuge to huge numbers of overwintering wading birds and wildfowl, as well as providing year-round habitats for many other birds and fish. Estuaries are places where rivers meet the sea. In most estuaries the heavier, denser salt water floods along the bottom of the channel, while the lighter fresh water flows in a layer above the salt. But in some, notably the estuaries of such rivers as the Severn, the Seine and the Amazon, and in the Bay of Fundy in eastern Canada, after low tide, salt water moves forward in a great surge or bore (sometimes called an eagre), mixing completely with the fresh water. As the river flows towards the sea, it picks up loose rocks, boulders and silt and carries them along in the strength of its flood; but as it nears the coast it lose the energy to transport heavy weights and meet the sea carrying only mud and silt suspended in the water. When the fresh water and sea water meet, the suspended particles of sediment are attracted to each other by a process known as flocculation; as the accumulating groups of sediments become bigger and heavier, they fall, and over a period of time the mud level is raised into banks. In the course of hundreds of years, a natural succession takes place around an estuary, from bare flat mud to mudbanks which over many years become salt marsh; in its turn over centuries the salt marsh endeavours to become firm land.

Wading birds feed mainly on crustaceans, worms and molluscs, and that is why there are so many of them around estuaries, especially in winter. All wading birds breed in the northern hemisphere and all are migratory; many cross the equator to overwinter. Britain and Ireland are sufficiently far north to provide breeding grounds for some waders, but also far enough south to be the overwintering grounds for others. Europe and America share many of the same species of shore birds, either as breeding species or as visitors.

Wading birds have a number of characteristics in common: all have long legs and long-toed feet in relation to their body size; many have long, slender wings, adapted to fast and long-range flight. In winter, most wading birds have drab plumage colours, affording camouflage against their habitat background of mud-flats, sandy beaches or estuaries. There are, of course, exceptions to this general rule: the woodcock retains its russet-barred camouflage throughout the year, blending perfectly with the undergrowth of damp woodlands in which it lives its secretive life. Glossy lapwings, gleaming purple-green, and speckled golden plovers gather on farmland, where they search for insects and worms, tough they are sometimes also seen on mud-flats and seashores during mild spells in winter.

Winter is a good time for watching wading birds probing for food, for observing their flight patterns and for noting their behaviour. Wading birds and waterfowl have developed routines which take advantage of any opportunity for feeding. The behaviour patterns of shore birds such as turnstones, curlews, oystercatchers, knots and dunlins are controlled by the cycle of the tides. At high tide these birds are forced off their mud-flat feeding grounds, and many gather at the top of the shore to sleep in tightly packed groups until the tide begins to ebb; but when the sea has covered the mid-tide zone, some oystercatchers and curlews fly to coastal pastures, where they join flocks of lapwings and golden plovers. The time of high water changes by roughly an hour each day and the height of the tide varies with the lunar cycle, yet the birds are able to predict accurately the time to leave the farmland, which may be some distance inland, and arrive on their newly exposed strip of mud-flat to resume feeding. Meanwhile, the birds which have been roosting on the upper shore start to feed as soon as the tide begins to ebb, moving down the shore as the sea retreats. The waders with the longest bills, such as the curlews and godwits, leave their roosts later, as their main sources of food – lugworms and ragworms – are found lower down the shore and therefore remain underwater longer.

Wading birds face various problems in winter, when bad weather can make feeding very difficult. Strong winds hamper feeding, as the sand or mud dries out quickly and the invertebrates remain deep in their burrows, not giving away their positions to birds which hunt by sight. A frost may cover the shore with a skin of ice that makes feeding impossible, or it may be so cold that the invertebrates become sluggish and remain inactive under the mud.

Opposite: the tracks left in the snow by birds and mammals.

Migrating Butterflies

It is difficult to imagine that the delicate fluttering of butterflies and moths could possibly enable the insects to migrate, but some species are stronger fliers than they appear and are quite capable of prolonged flight.

But how do migrating butterflies navigate? The answer is that they fly only during the warmest part of the day and when the sun in shining; detailed study has shown that they maintain a constant angle to the point on the horizon directly below the sun, known as the azimuth. Butterflies of temperate climates differ from birds, bees and tropical butterflies in that they do not compensate for the movement of the sun across the horizon. So although they gradually make their way across country in a more or less constant geographical direction, their flight path forms a series of gentle curves as they follow the sun. In this way a butterfly increases the area it flies over, making it more likely that it will find a habitat in which its larval plants may grow − in other words, a suitable place for a female to lay her eggs.

The monarch is the most famous of the migrating butterflies, because it makes a migration involving a similar return journey to those of migrating birds. At least part of that return journey is made by the same butterflies that travelled on the outward leg, as well as by their offspring − monarchs live comparatively long adult lives − up to twelve months.

Throughout the summer the monarch is a common sight in the gardens and countryside of North America, but in late summer and early autumn it begins its journey south. This migration flight, from the Great Lakes in the north to Texas or the Gulf of Mexico in the south, covers between 2000 and 3000 km (1250–1850 miles). Many of the towns on the monarch's flight path have festivals or carnivals to celebrate the arrival of the butterflies. I have seen clouds of them

flying southwards through Texas, with steady wing-beats. They were about 4–6 metres (15–20 feet) above the ground and travelled at about 17 km (11 miles) an hour. It was a never-to-be-forgotten sight.

The monarchs that reach Mexico spend the winter as free-flying, reproductive butterflies; they die within a few weeks of beginning to reproduce and it is their offspring that make the return flight north in the spring. The butterflies that do not fly far enough south to avoid being caught in a cold weather zone form spectacular, colourful 'butterfly trees', clustering together on evergreens so that the trees are completely festooned with roosting butterflies. In some forests in northern Mexico and southern California, populations of hundreds of millions of monarch butterflies can be found clinging to trees and delighting the eyes of those who go to see them.

Then, from the beginning of March, most of the monarchs fly north, the females laying eggs as they go. During autumn and winter, they are not reproductively active, so they do not have to use up energy courting or laying eggs – they need only feed, rest and build up strength for their journey.

Opposite: hybernating hedgehog

Camouflage Dress –

As the days become shorter, animals begin to grow thicker coats and some change the colour of their fur or feathers from summer hues to winter white. Animals which become paler in winter lives in areas where that season is hard and there is a strong likelihood of the ground being covered in snow, so camouflage is almost certainly the reason for the change.

Mountain or blue hares, which live at high altitudes and high latitudes, crouch in a shallow form or scrape amongst the heather or on a more open hillside. If they retained their grey-brown pelage in winter they might easily fall victim to passing birds of prey. In October, the lighter-weight male apparently begins to feel the cold first and starts to change to a white winter coat; the heavier female follows suit when she feels cold. First the furred hind feet become white, and gradually the colour change moves over the body, reaching the head last of all. Only the tips of the ears remain black. The hare does not moult its autumn coat until its winter coat is fully grown, so there is always protection from the cold;

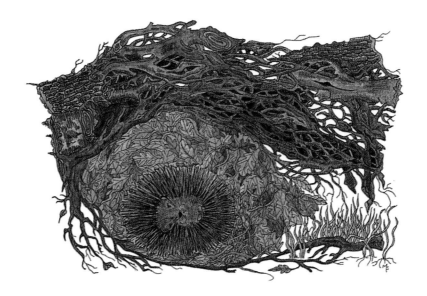

the white winter fur is thicker and longer than the autumn coat, and there is lots of underfur to keep out icy winds. The Peak District, where I live, is the only place in England where mountain hares are to be found. They were introduced into this area from Scotland in the 1860s and soon found the high moorland to their liking, so the population increased. They are easy to see in snow-free conditions, but as soon as the first snow falls, they are almost perfectly camouflaged, crouching as still as can be in their form and only leaping away at the last minute to avoid being stepped on. During the short winter days they feed on heather and cotton grass, digging through the soft snow if necessary to reach the vegetation buried beneath it. However, if the snow becomes ice-crusted or is very deep, they are unable to dig down and have to look for juniper, willow or rowan twigs to nibble. When grazing, they keep their backs to the wind and feed in a half circle, moving slowly forwards about 30 cm (1 ft) at a time. During storms, mountain hares gather into large groups on the sheltered side of ridges, making scrapes in the snow for shelter. Many die of starvation in prolonged, severe winters.

Mountain hares can be found in Ireland, Scotland, northern parts of Europe and Asia, and in the Alps. In Alaska, Canada and mountainous regions of the continental United States there is a similar creature called the snowshoe, which changes from summer brown to winter buff, a colour that undoubtedly has camouflage value.

Stoats are widespread in the northern hemisphere. In the southern parts of their range they keep their chestnut-brown colouring throughout the year. Those living further north may become paler in winter, but the stoats of the far north change their coat to that of ermine – white with a black tail-tip – which gives them camouflage when they stalk their prey. The stoat is a fierce animal with little to fear from predators – although adults are occasionally taken by larger mammals, hawks and owls, so the white pelage may act in a defensive way, too. Both red and grey squirrels have paler coats in winter, and deer moult to a more subdued shade of brown for the winter period.

The Arctic regions of Europe, Asia and North America have short summers, when lichens, mosses and many flowering plants flourish on the tundra and provide food for

A stoat in its characteristic winter livery

herbivores. During the long, cold winter months, ice and snow cover much of the land and there are few animals to be seen. However, surviving on these frozen wastes are three mammals which change the colour of their fur to camouflage themselves – the lemming, the Arctic fox and the Arctic hare.

Lemmings are preyed on by the Arctic fox and the snowy owl, so they try to keep a low profile by travelling about along runways close to the ground, beneath the snow. It is much warmer under the snow than out in the open, and these small, fat, guinea pig-like rodents trot along their snow-topped corridors nibbling the vegetation. When an Arctic fox becomes aware of their presence, it pounces, stiff-legged, trying to force the lemmings out of their tunnels, or it digs deep into the snow in an attempt to scoop its prey out.

While the Arctic fox is hunting in this way, it is often watched by a snowy owl which, seeing the fox catch a lemming, will fly down and try to drive it away from the kill. Lemmings form a major part of the diet of the Arctic fox and the snowy owl; so much so, that the numbers of the predators fluctuate with the availability of lemmings.

The Arctic fox is a rounder, sturdier animal than the red fox.

Its nose is less pointed and its ears are shorter and more rounded; these are adaptations to reduce the risk of frostbite in the intense cold. The Arctic fox is able to withstand temperatures as low as –50°C (–58°F). During the short summer, it is greyish brown in colour, and this changes to a creamy white as winter approaches. Like the red fox, the Arctic fox is flexible in its behaviour, travelling long distances to find food and hunting by day or by night. Any food that can't be eaten at once is stored in a hole in the snow, or in a crevice of rock.

Arctic foxes also hunt for Arctic hares, which are camouflaged in winter-white fur. These hares have great difficulty in finding food when snows covers the tundra; they must dig deep into the snow in an attempt to find leaves to keep them from starving. The few leaves that the hares find are tough and, although they supplement these with lichen nibbled from rocks, it is a poor diet in the freezing temperatures. All the time the hares are searching for food they must watch out for predators and they sometimes gather in large groups, probably because there is safety in numbers: with any luck, at least one pair of eyes will see the approach of danger and warn the others. In these conditions only the fittest animals are able to survive.

Opposite: lemmings under their blanket of snow

The Deep Sleep of Hibernation

When an animal finds itself in a cold environment it has to develop ways of keeping itself warm.

The key structure involved in the temperature regulation of warm-blooded animals is the skin. When an animal is exposed to the cold, heat will be lost from the body, but the body will respond in four ways to the potential heat loss. Firstly, fat stored under the skin acts as an insulator and

reduces heat loss from the body. Animals which live in very cold habitats, such as polar bears and seals, have a very thick layer of this subcutaneous fat. Secondly, hair is raised and brought into a more or less vertical position, trapping air in the space between the hairs. This air is warmed by the body and forms an insulating layer around the animal. When a bird fluffs its feathers out on a cold winter's day, it is trapping air around its body.

Thirdly, in cold weather blood is diverted from the surface of the skin to the deeper layers when blood vessels in the skin constrict; this reduces loss of heat from the blood to the surrounding atmosphere. When this happens we go pale, or 'blue', with cold. Arctic explorers and mountaineers may be exposed to extreme cold for so long that skin cells die, resulting in frostbite due to prolonged absence of blood from the skin's surface.

And finally, extra heat is produced by an increase in the metabolic rate which causes shivering and 'gooseflesh'. Vigorous exercise creates extra heat, too: even stamping our feet helps us to keep warm if we are standing around in the cold. In winter, as much as 40 per cent of the energy provided by the food we eat may be used in generating heat when we are at rest.

The centre for controlling body temperature is a small area in the brain called the hypothalamus, which acts as a thermostat. But there comes a point when the body's ability to regulate its temperature breaks down. There is a critical temperature range which varies from species to species. If the temperature rises above the upper critical point, the animal dies of heat; below the lower critical point, it dies of cold. Animals which live in cold environments are therefore adapted to withstand lower temperatures than animals living in a warm climate. If man had not developed the ability to make clothes, he would not have been able to live in the temperate areas of the world – unless he had seasonally migrated or hibernated – because human beings have a low critical temperature level, not much below that of a desert rat!

As the low critical temperature is approached, the metabolic rate of the body increases. This means that more energy has to be used and more food is needed to fuel the energy. But if an animal can find a way of slowing its metabolic rate, it will not be under the same pressure to find food during winter when supplies are scarce. This is what happens during hibernation. The animal goes into a deep sleep. Its metabolic rate falls to the minimum needed to keep it alive; its body temperature drops; its heartbeat slows and breathing almost stops. It enters a state of suspended animation, becoming stiff and cold, almost as if it were dead. Temperature regulation does not stop completely, but the acceptable minimum is much lower than usual – rather like turning a thermostat down to a lower setting to save fuel.

All animals have to eat large amounts of food in late summer and early autumn in order to build up fat and so increase their chances of winter survival. Hibernators must have particularly large stores of fat in their body, to keep their systems ticking over during their long sleep. In some years, if the weather is bad in late summer and early autumn, hibernators cannot find enough food to increase their fat reserves to a safe level and they may die before the end of winter.

Hibernating mammals usually allow their body temperature to fall to that of their surroundings, so that their temperature fluctuates as the air temperature rises and falls. But if the air temperature falls to below freezing point, the hibernator's body functions switch on again, either to keep the body from freezing or to arouse the animal into activity to warm itself up. Arousal from hibernating sleep occurs quite often and means that the animals need to eat in order to fuel the extra energy they are using. On mild winter nights hedgehogs snuffle around looking for food and you may even have seen bats hunting winter moths.

Bees

In Britain, honey bees are the first bees to appear in spring. They are followed by the first queen bumble bees and then the early solitary bees. Although these bees have varied tongue lengths, they all feed from the nectar and pollen of the goat willow and from the early flowers of coltsfoot and dandelion.

Solitary bees overwinter as pupae, tucked up in holes in well-drained soil, in walls or in wood, where they are put as eggs by a mother who does not survive long enough to see her offspring.

Each autumn, bumble bee colonies die of cold and starvation, leaving behind fertilized queens, who hibernate alone throughout the winter, to establish new colonies in spring. The young bumble bee queen chooses a site for hibernation in autumn; it is often a north-facing bank which will not be warmed by the winter sun, so that she will not wake up too early. Here she burrows several centimetres (an inch or two) into the soil and overwinters, living on accumulated fat. By the time the soil temperature rises in spring, most of this food reserve has been used up and the bee emerges to sun herself, warming her muscles before foraging for pollen and nectar among the early flowers; the food helps her ovaries begin to develop.

Look out for the large bumble bee queens visiting the flowers of pussy willow, white deadnettle or flowering currant; and

The rich habitat provided by a tree stump

watch as the bees search for a suitable nesting site, flying to and fro over banks and rough ground, exploring holes and disappearing under tussocks of grass. Bumble bee queens look for established nest sites which will save them time and energy; they seem to favour old mouse holes and vole holes and will sometimes be persuaded to nest in an upturned earthenware plant pot if it has some mousey-smelling nesting material in it. Having prepared a suitable site, the queen bumble bee begins to found a colony of bees that will forage for pollen and nectar – and so pollinate flowers – until autumn.

The Emergence of Woodland

About 10,000 years ago, at the end of the last Ice Age, most of Britain and northern Europe was tundra, frozen for much of the year but supporting low-growing plants such as lichen, mosses, bilberry and juniper. At this time, Britain was still joined to the continent of Europe so, as the ice sheet gradually retreated northwards and the summers became warmer and the winters less severe, plant life began to spread from the southern parts of Europe which had not been ice bound.

The first real trees to grow were very hardy: birch, rowan, hazel, willow and Scots pine. As the climate improved, the pine-dominated woodlands spread northwards. The animals associated with these woodlands moved northwards too, probably including red squirrels, red deer, wild boar and wolves.

The climate continued to improve, enabling elm, alder, oak, beech and small-leaved lime trees to replace the Scots pine. The pines were gradually driven further and further north to the Scottish Highlands, where their descendants grow today in conditions too harsh for other trees to compete.

Most woodland areas now have one or two species of trees that outnumber the others. The tree that is present in the largest numbers is called the dominant species. These dominant trees influence all other plant life in the wood, and the plant life in turn influences the animal life. If there are two species in more or less equal numbers, they are 'co-dominant'. There are several types of woodland, depending on the local soil and climate. These include damp oak-wood, dry oak-wood, ash-wood, beech-wood, birch-wood, alder carr and plantations of mixed woodland.

The most common woodland type in Britain is dominated by oak. Throughout the last few centuries the number of oak-woods has been greatly influenced by the economy. Oak timber is highly valued for house- and ship-building; many oak trees were planted and the woodlands were managed for timber and for the oak bark, which provided tannic acid for the growing tanning industry.

There are two species of native British oak, both found throughout the country. The common or pedunculate oak, *Quercus robur*, prefers the heavy clay soils of the lowlands, while the durmast or sessile oak, *Quercus petraea*, favours the shallow, lighter soil of the uplands.

Oak trees have both male and female flowers, which open in late spring just after the leaves have expanded. Pedunculate oak has very short-stemmed leaves which have ear-like (auriculate) lobes at the base and are quite smooth in texture underneath. The twigs are rugged and the oval leaf buds are spirally arranged, with a cluster of buds at the tip. The female flowers on their long stalks are carried near the tips of the twigs, and the male catkins hang further back. The acorns of this oak are carried on long stalks; these are the peduncles which give the species its common name.

Opposite: the intriguing galls found on a variety of trees

Sessile means stalkless, and the acorns of *Quercus petraea* are borne on very, very short stalks. The female flowers are carried in the leaf axils near the tips of the twigs, and the male flowers hang further back, in a similar way to those of the pedunculate oak. The leaves of the sessile oak have long stalks, and the leaf base is tapered, lacking the auricles of the pedunculate oak. The leaves are downy beneath.

Life in the Woodland

The competition for food in woodland is very fierce particularly between members of the same species, so, before the breeding season, many birds stake out a territory and defend it strongly. The territory includes the nest and the feeding ground around it. Song birds proclaim their territory by perching on a song post and singing a distinctive song. The holding of territories ensures that birds are spread out, so sharing out the available food.

Woods are full of hidden life, much of which is active only at dawn, at dusk and after dark; so when you walk through a wood you will be lucky if you see any animals. They will have heard you coming, and may even lurk in a safe place to watch you walk by.

Invertebrates are a very important part of life in a woodland. They are food for several small mammals and for birds; most seed-eating birds feed their nestlings on insects until the young birds can manage harder food and are able to fly to water to drink.

A log in a moist part of a shady wood is a good place to watch invertebrate life. Moss often grows on the bark of trees – looked at through a magnifying glass it looks like a miniature jungle through which moss snails roam and red soil mites and pseudoscorpions hunt. Mesh web spiders live

in the cracks in loose bark, with a tangled surface web designed to catch crawling insects. Gallery patterns may be a sign that bark beetles have moved in.

Bark beetles are often the first occupants of a dead tree. The adult beetle gnaw through the outer bark and tunnel a little gallery where they mate. The female elongates the pairing gallery, gnawing tiny niches at intervals along its walls and putting an egg into each niche. When the eggs hatch, each larva gnaws at its own gallery, extending outwards and more or less at right angles to the main one. As the larvae grow, the galleries increase in width to accommodate their little fat bodies, until they finally end in pupal cells. The beetles that emerge gnaw a short tunnel out of the bark, living exit holes that are visible to the careful observer.

These activities loosen the bark of the tree, making it possible for other creatures to get in. Woodlice enjoy this habitat; they eat decaying vegetation, fungi and wood, and they need to live in damp conditions their body covering is not waterproof and they dry out in open, sunny places. Female woodlice do not lay their eggs and leave them hidden; instead they keep them in pockets underneath their body, where the young hatch.

Bee flowers

Pollen is a vital source of food for flower-visiting insects. Pollen contain proteins, fats, sugar, vitamins and minerals. So when animals eat pollen, they absorb essential materials for growth and repair to their body cells. Bees are the chief collectors of pollen, as they feed it to their young.

Wind-dispersed pollen grains have to be small and smooth to remain airborne, Insect-dispersed pollen grains are often spiky or sticky in order to cling more easily to their

pollinators; the pollinators are correspondingly hairy. There are various ways in which bees transport pollen back to their nest or hive. Some, such as one of the solitary bees in the genus *Prosopis*, are shiny, almost hairless bees; they carry pollen mixed with nectar in their crop, then it is regurgitated when they reach the nest. Most species of bees carry pollen on the outside of their bodies, between hairs that are especially adapted for the purpose. Some, such as the leaf-cutter bees, have their undersides covered with specialized hairs which curve back stiffly towards their rear ends.

Flowers adapted to pollination by bees open during the day, but within this period the flowers have their own particular 'opening hours'. Broad beans, for example, open first in the afternoon between noon and 2 pm; dandelions open within half an hour of the sun striking them and begin to close three hours later; the common name of *Tragopogon pratensis* is Jack-go-to-bed-at-noon, as this is the time when the flower closes. Many species are so specific in their behaviour that it is possible to work out a floral clock using flower times. This time schedule is geared to the behaviour of bees, who are stimulated to forage mainly during periods of high light intensity.

Bee flowers are found in various shades of blue, purple, red-purple, yellow and orange, which are all within the colour range of bees. Pure red is rare except in poppies; these, together with many white and yellow flowers, reflect ultra violet, which attracts bees, who do not see the colour red.

Many flowers which look identical to the human eye have varying ultra-violet patterns on them; these are easily seen by bees, who use the patterns as nectar guides. For us there is a great contrast between the bright flowers and the green leaves; if green leaves are photographed using a lens which shows ultra violet, they appear grey. Bees probably see flowers as coloured mosaic patterns on a grey background.

Springtime Rituals: Frogs & Toads

Frogs, toads and newts are amphibians: animals who live on land but breed in water. They are three or four years old before they are sexually developed. Sometimes a young frog will join the *melée* at a breeding site, but unless he is very 'butch' he will be pushed to one side as the mature males are so strong and determined.

Common frogs usually have a smooth skin, but in the breeding season the females develop pearly granules on their sides. At this time, the male frog's thumbs thicken with nuptial pads of dark, rough skin which enable him to hold his slippery companion firmly whilst mating. Common toads have warty skins and the males develop dark nuptial pads on the three inner fingers in the breeding season.

Frogs emerge from hibernation some time towards the end of winter or beginning of spring, depending on the weather. The males usually arrive at the spawning site first, and begin calling for the females; when the females arrive there is great excitement and competition among the many males to lay claim to one of the less numerous females. The sexual urge is so strong that a male frog may pinion a fish, a stick or another male frog in his frenzied arms. Fortunately, a male who is so held by another male is able to escape the clutches by emitting a high-pitched release call, which is quite different to the deep croak of the mating call, and the grappled male is promptly set free with little more than his ego ruffled!

The successful male frog, having so inelegantly jumped on to the back of a female, wraps his forelimbs around her body, just below her armpits, and hangs on. the pair may be in this position of amplexus for some time before the female begins to lay. About 2,000 eggs slide into the water, and the male releases his sperm over them as they leave the female's body.

The envelope of jelly which surrounds each one begins to swell, so insulating and protecting the egg. At first the spawn sinks down into the water, but soon the gelatinous mass rises to the surface.

The common toad is later in rousing from hibernation, and may be a month behind the frogs in making for the breeding sites. The journey to the preferred water, chosen because it is deep, may be long and hazardous. The males start out before the females, but often their paths meet and many female toads arrive at their chosen pond with a male already in amplexus. A male toad has no permanent right to the female he has grabbed. He may be unseated by a larger, stronger male; the bigger the toad, the deeper and more resonant his voice, and such males are seldom interfered with. The female extrudes her 5,000 or more eggs in a long rope, and the male fertilizes them as they are shed; the egg rope is carefully entwined around the stems of water plants, where the tadpoles soon begin to develop.

Toad tadpoles are poisonous to fish, newts and some other predators, but they face many hazards and only a few toad or frog tadpoles from each batch of eggs finally become adults.

The eggs develop into tadpoles in two or three weeks, depending on the water temperature. There may be some infertile eggs; these will turn grey and fail to change shape. Soon each wriggling tadpole will digest its surrounding jelly, and the adhesive organ, in the region of the developing mouth, will enable it to cling to other spawn or to water plants or stones.

While the mouth is forming, the tadpole is nourished by the remains of the yolk sac in its stomach. When the mouth has formed, the tadpole begins to eat algae and soft leaf tissue, breathing by means of three external gills. These gills soon become covered by a flap of skin. The tadpole then breathes through a spiracle, an air vent, in the left-hand side; this is connected to an internal gill cavity.

Usually, hind leg stumps appear after five weeks. Two weeks after the legs appear, toes develop on the feet. At about this time the tadpoles stop being plant eaters and need to eat meat. At about eight weeks, lungs develop and the tadpoles begin to gulp air. The front legs begin to show by about week ten and the tail is slowly absorbed.

One-parent Family: Three-spined Stickleback

The three-spined stickleback is a lively little fish which grows to a length of 9 cm (3½ in). Its dorsal fins consist of three separate stiff spines which are raised in fear or aggression. The body does not have scales; instead it hasan armour of body plates.

In spring, the male stickleback develops his breeding colours: his throat and belly become red, his eyes blue and his back a shimmering blue-green. Each male isolates himself and selects a territory which he defends fiercely. He excavates a saucer-shaped depression by sucking mouthfuls of sand or silt from the bottom of his pond or stream habitat and spitting it out away from the site. Then he gathers bits of pond weed from around his territory and puts them into the depression; he sticks them together with a kidney secretion which is released when he presses himself against the gathered vegetation. After much gathering, packing and gluing, the nest mound is ready and the male wriggles into it to make a tunnel through the middle.

Meanwhile the female sticklebacks, heavy with eggs, become interested in the nest; but the male drives them away harshly.

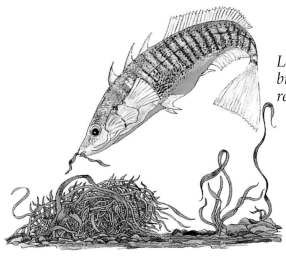

Left. The male stickleback builds a nest in spring in readiness for mating.

Opposite. The zigzag courtship dance is a series of interactions. The female arrives - the fish dance - the male courts - the male leads - the female follows - the male shows her the next - the female enters and spawns - the male fertilizes the eggs and drives the female away.

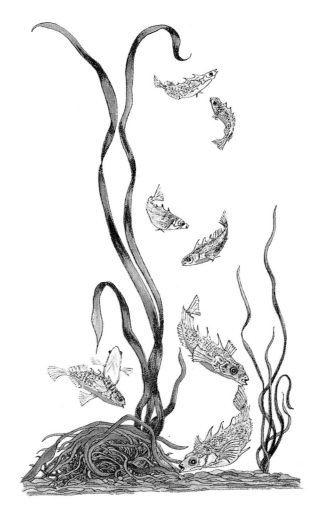

This is part of the selection process; the male is looking for females who are very sexually motivated, and his aggressive manner frightens away the faint-hearted.

When a male is ready to take a female to his nest, he courts the fish of his choice and they perform a zigzag dance. The dance sequence is a chain of interactions between the male and the female, in which neither will proceed from one act to another unless suitable response actions are made. The male will not lead a female to his nest unless every step in the set routine has been carried out; then he entices her down. He points at the entrance with his head and chivvies the female fish into the tunnel. When she enters, the male butts her sides and trembles to stimulate her spawning; she lays her eggs, and he follows her to fertilize them by shedding milt (sperm) into the water around the eggs. The female is driven away by the male, who then stays on guard, fanning the water with his tail to make sure the water is well supplied with oxygen. Occasionally a water snail may wander over the nest; if it is small, the male stickleback will carry it away. If the snail is large it poses a bit of a problem, but vigorous prodding causes it to withdraw into its shell, and then it is easily pushed away from the nest to the stickleback's satisfaction.

After a week or so, depending on the water temperature, the eggs hatch. The male prevents the fry from straying far; if any do wander off, he sucks them into his mouth and spits them back into the nest. The little sticklebacks are soon big enough to fend for themselves and they disperse.

Ruthless Killers: Great Diving Beetles

Great diving beetles (see opposite), are amazing: they are capable of flying from pond to pond, yet are totally at home under water. The beetle's oval body is dark green above and bright yellow below, with a yellow body trim and legs. The

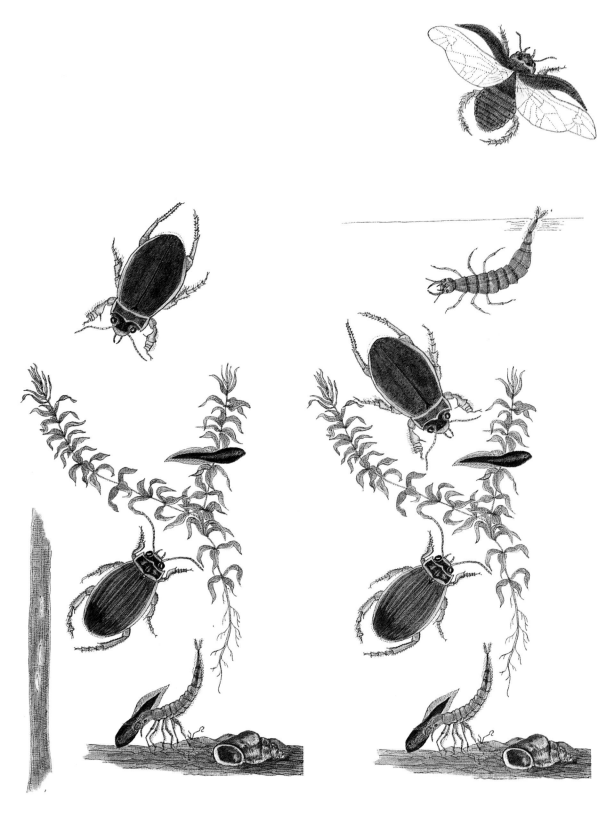

male has smooth elytra (wing cases) and sucker pads on his front legs, while the female has grooved elytra and no sucker pads. The eyes of both sexes are light and bright, situated at the side of the head so that the beetle can see above and below its body. Each eye has about 9,000 tiny units called facets and the beetles miss very little; they are fierce and greedy predators.

The hind legs are fringed with long, stiff hairs which spread out during the 'pull' stroke and flatten during the 'return' stroke, so 'feathering' the rowing legs and enabling the beetles to swim strongly.

Breathing takes place at the water surface where the beetle sticks out its back end, raises the elytra slightly and takes in air through large spiracles or air vents. When the beetle returns underwater, it appears to have a silvery end to its body. This air bubble is slowly used up. The warmer the water, the less oxygen there is in it and the more rapidly diffusion will take place.

Great diving beetles have a number of mechanisms which enable them to defend themselves against predators: in addition to a pair of sharp spikes on their undersides, they have the ability to produce an unpleasant-smelling nerve poison from glands on the thorax - enough to kill a frog!

The females are very productive and lay white cigar-shaped eggs about 6 mm (1/4 in) long, inserting them into the stems of water plants. The larvae that emerge from the eggs are even more aggressive than their parents: so fierce, in fact, that they have earned the name 'water tigers'.

Insects on the Hop

One of the great joys of
lying in a meadow, watching
and listening, is the constant
'chirping' of grasshoppers;
the game is trying to spot
them!

Grasshoppers and crickets
belong to the order
Orthoptera, a word which
means straight-winged and
refers to the narrow forewings
which lie along the sides of
the body of the insect.

Bush crickets have long
antennae - often longer
than the body -- and are
sometimes called long-horned
grasshoppers. The females have
broad, sabre-like ovipositors
and are thus differentiated from
the males. Bush crickets are
partly carnivorous and, as
their name suggests, they
are often found in bushes
or in taller herbage than
grasshoppers.

Male bush crickets sing
by rubbing their wing bases
together. It is a file and
scraper mechanism, like
drawing a comb over a card;
the file is on the left forewing

while the hind edge of the right forewing forms the scraper. The sounds are picked up by tiny drum-like membranes, tympanal organs, on the front legs.

Grasshoppers have short antennae and are sometimes called short-horned grasshoppers, which distinguishes them from bush crickets. Grasshoppers are vegetarian, eating leaves and grass, and are usually found in low-growing vegetation where the adults chirp merrily, rubbing the row of pegs on the inner side of the large tigh against the prominent veins of the forewing on each side. Each species has its own particular song; the males call stridently while the females have a quieter chirp. Grasshopper 'ears' are at the base of the first abdominal segment on each side of the body.

Most grasshoppers and crickets have one generation a year; the egg is the overwintering stage. The eggs of crickets are laid singly, while those of grasshoppers are laid in groups, surrounded by a pod of earth mixed with a glandular secretion.

The young insect, a nymph, is creamy white and enclosed in a thin, transparent sac. During late spring the nymph wriggles out of the sac, sheds its skin and emerges as a tiny wingless replica of the adult. As the nymph feeds and grows, it becomes too big for its skin and has to moult. The number of instars varies between species. After each moult, the little grasshopper is larger and a stage nearer to becoming an adult. There is no pupation stage in this form of development, which is called incomplete metamorphosis. After the final moult the insect is a mature adult, ready to reproduce.

A Short, Hard Life – Solitary Wasps

Anything you hear about the building behaviour of wasps, bees and ants refers to the female, as the male, apart from mating, doesn't do anything constructive. Among highly developed insects, the females ensure the survival of their young by building and stocking a shelter. 'Building' may simply mean making a hole in the ground, but the ingenuity of some of these structures is wonderful.

Many wasp species live solitary lives, and although they are common they often remain unnoticed. After mating, the males either die or stay around for a while sipping nectar, while the females work very hard to ensure that the species survives. Solitary wasps feed their larvae on whole insects which are alive but paralyzed by the wasp's sting. Each wasp species specializes in a particular prey, which may be caterpillars, flies, weevils, bees, aphids or spiders.

Many solitary wasps are known as 'digger' wasps because they excavate their nests in light, sandy soil, working with their mouth parts as grabbers and their feet as rakes. Each individual egg has its own nest cavity.

The black and red solitary wasp *Ammophila pubescens* is about 2cm (just under an inch) long and likes to dig in sandy soil where pine trees grow. After mating, the insect searches for a nest site, flying low and stopping every now and again to run over the ground and scratch at likely places, until she finds loose sandy soil that is workable. She loosens the soil with her mandibles (mouth parts) and carries a load away, holding it between her forelegs and thorax (chest). All the soil excavated is carried away like this; by scattering it around she avoids making a heap outside the nest which would advertise her whereabouts to parasites.

The wasp digs until the shaft is 2 or 3 cm (about an inch)

deep with a rounded cell at the bottom, making the nest sock-shaped. She searches about for a pebble or stick which will fit into the opening of the finished shaft, using her open jaw to measure, since this is the span of the mouth of the shaft. She may have to try several plugs before she finds one to her satisfaction. After protecting her nest from unwelcome visitors, the wasp flies above the site and memorizes the landmarks – maybe a pine cone or stick close to the nest – then she goes caterpillar hunting. Where there are pine trees, she will probably find pine looper or pine beauty caterpillars. Having found her prey, she paralyzes in with her sting and with great effort transports it to her nest; she may be able to fly with it, or she may have to drag it part or all of the way.

She next has to reopen the shaft and then, creeping backwards, she drags the caterpillar down into the nest, where she deposits an egg on it; then she closes the shaft as before and begins to excavate another nest, where shewill lay another egg. She does this several times.

The wasp inspects her nests each morning, unsealing each one and sealing it up again. When she sees a larva has hatched, she provides it will more caterpillar food; then when it reaches a certain size, she pops a number of caterpillars into the nest and seals up the shaft with great care for the last time, leaving the larvae to pupate and overwinter.

This wasp keeps up her energy by taking nectar from flowers with shallow nectaries and by licking the body fluids from her caterpillar prey. She appears to spend the hours of darkness among plant stems.

Paper Makers: Social Wasps

The wasps with whom everyone is familiar are the black and yellow insects with bad tempers and painful stings. These are the social wasps living in annual communities with one fertilized queen who is the mother of them all.

There are seven species of social wasp in the British Isles: these include the hornet, which is a brown and gold wood wasp and is quite uncommon. There are many more wasp species in Europe.

Adult wasps of all species eat only sweet things such as nectar, honeydew and ripe fruit. Wasp larvae eat flesh which has been chewed and softened by the worker wasps; so wasps of all kinds are useful as scavengers, disposing of small corpses as well as rounding up caterpillar and fly pests to feed to their young.

The life-cycle of the social wasp goes like this. In early spring, young, fertilized queen wasps emerge from hibernation and look for a suitable nesting site. Common, German and red wasps look for empty mouse holes, convenient lofts and sheds. Norwegian and tree wasps hang their nests from bushes or in the hollows of trees; the hornet uses a tree hole; while the cuckoo wasp puts her eggs into the nest of the red wasp (which is really black and yellow like the others).

The queen wasp gathers building material to build her nest. She looks for the dry, sound wood of fences and trees which she rasps off with very strong jaws. Then she chews it and it mixes with her saliva to form wasp paper. On quiet days in spring it is easy to hear this wasp activity.

Using the damp wasp paper, the queen makes a strong stem. From this, she builds a few cells, her only tools being her mouth parts and her front legs. The queen then begins to lay, fastening an egg into each downward-pointing cell. Before the larvae hatch, the queen surrounds the tiny nest with a protective wasp-paper envelope, leaving only a flight hole at the bottom. When the larvae hatch from the eggs, the queen feeds them on well-chewed flesh. About two weeks later, each larva spins a silk top to its cell and pupates, soon to emerge as a worker wasp.

Gradually the workers take over the running of the nest, leaving the queen free to continue laying eggs. They enlarge the nest and forage for food for the young, and by late summer there are thousands of wasps in the colony. Larger cells are made at this time, in which males and potential queens are raised; these leave the nest to mate, and the young fertilized queens eat well to prepare for hibernation.

Meanwhile, the old queen stops laying, so the workers haven't any work to do. They indulge themselves by eating all the sweet things they can find. This is the time when we find wasps a nuisance.

The old queen slowly dies of starvation and, as the weather gets colder, the rest of the colony dies too, leaving the hibernating queen to start again in spring.

Opposite: Deciphering the tracks and traces left by animals in the snow can be fascinating. A track means a set of footprints, while a trace may be any sign of a creature's presence, such as feathers, a dropping or some partly eaten food. With a bit of practice, you will be able to deduce which animal has left each clue.

Ivy

Shade-loving plants will grow around the roots of the thicket-forming plants. Ivy is a very useful plant to animals who nest among its branches, hibernate in its protection, hide from predators and hunt for food. Ivy is the last plant to flower in the year, and is pollinated by wasps and flies. The berries are eaten by birds, who are glad of food in the depths of winter.

The holly blue butterfly often uses ivy as a food plant. The first holly blues emerge in the middle of spring, and within a few weeks they lay their eggs in developing holly flowers. The caterpillars soon hatch and eat the holly flowers and any of their kin that they encounter. the full, fat caterpillars pupate in the middle of summer, hanging from holly leaves. The second batch of adults are on the wing a month later and, as there aren't any holly flowers to lay eggs in, the butterflies choose ivy buds as food for their young. The caterpillars pupate in the ivy through the winter.

Caught in a Rock Pool

When I go to a beach, I always look around for a rock pool. Kneeling down and gazing into the beautiful under-sea garden with its swimming, darting or creeping inhabitants is a wonderful treat.

Shrimps and prawns live on an assortment of food, from bits of seaweed and dead creatures to small live prey. Shrimps are mainly nocturnal, but prawns are usually to be seen swimming in a rock pool, beating the water by tucking up the ten walking legs and bending back the feelers. The prawn swims slowly along, scavenging for food, but you only have to draw your finger over the water surface to see it shoot backwards paddling hard with its tail fan and darting away. I have been lucky enough to see a prawn moulting; they have to shed their exoskeleton every two weeks or so in the summer. The outgrown shell splits down the back, then the prawn humps its back and pushes outwards. It takes about two days for its new shell to harden, which is a long time to be vulnerable when predators lurk all around and cold strike at any moment.

One way to tell a prawn from a shrimp is to look at its pincers. The common prawn has the largest pair of pincers on the second pair of walking legs, while the common shrimp has the largest pincers on the first pair of walking legs. Also the common prawn has a beak, or rostrum, sticking forward out of the head between the eyes, but shrimps have only a small point or none at all.

Below: colourful sea anemones extent their tentacles to capture prey.

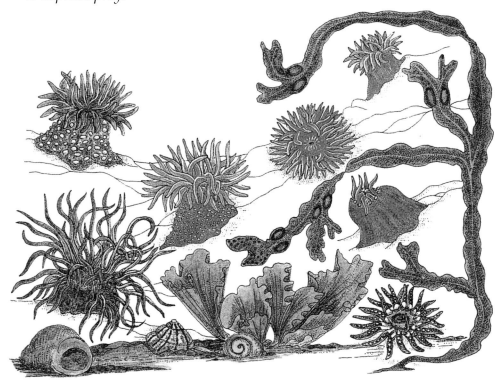

93